LANDING YOUR FIRST PUBLICATION

*the writing prompts + publication strategy
for writers who refuse to rely on luck*

▼

Mandy Wallace

*To Nathan Wallace, who always supports
me, and to everyone who encouraged
me to finally create this effing book*

CONTENTS

Introduction

THE STRATEGY

The Strategy

▼

SCREW LUCK

"Write a short story every week. It's not possible to write 52 bad short stories in a row." —Ray Bradbury

So much about becoming a writer feels like it's left to chance. Like only the lucky get to see their work in print. Only the lucky get to live the creative dream. Only the lucky end up in the right place at the right time to get their work published or to meet the right people in the writing business.

But here's the thing. *Writer* is just a career title—one in a healthy industry that uncounted people claim. So what if breaking into professional publication isn't really so much about chance? At the risk of diminishing the magic and romance of the writer life, what if breaking into publication is more about following the same system that all the published authors before you have followed?

Acclaimed science fiction writer, Ray Bradbury, said: "Write a short story every week. It's not possible to write 52 bad short stories in a row."

This author quote is more than it seems. It hides a secret strategy for any writing hopeful who wants to get published. Now if you collect author quotes like I do, this might seem like just a few more run-of-the-mill words of encouragement for new writers. And words of encouragement are nice for keeping us on the path to our publication goals, but it's strategy that will get us there.

I almost missed the magic in this quote from Bradbury. I saved it to a Pinterest board along with a hundred other author quotes I've forgotten.

But something about this quote stuck with me. And then gnawed at me. And the more I ran it over in my mind in the coming days, the more I saw a hidden strategy sprouting up in the spaces between Bradbury's words.

This book is that strategy realized.

Like Bradbury's quote, this book is more than it seems. More than a simple set of writing prompts, it's a step-by-step publication system with all the tools and resources you'll need to buff up your writing skills and submit your stories the right way—in a way that finally renders Chance powerless and gets Luck working *for* your writing dreams instead of against them.

We're not going to cover things like narrative theory or voice or point of view. Plenty of books on writing do this already and do it well. If you're like me, you own or have read towers of books like those. And, if you're like me in this too, those books can overcomplicate what should be simple when you're feeling blocked, just starting out, or are overwhelmed by "the rules."

Instead, we're just going to get you writing and submitting work. Without worry. Without editing yourself. And definitely without overthinking it.

This is a book of strategy. Strategy is powerful. It's what transforms your writing dreams from the empty goals and wishes of every starry-eyed hopeful out there into the sure path to published writer. Your writing dreams deserve more than wishing. They deserve a sure thing. They deserve a strategic publication system.

With a publication system like this one, it's possible to finally take your writing dreams into your own hands, using a method that's gotten so many successful authors where you want to be.

So screw luck. Instead, let's play to the numbers until fate gets the point and rolls over.

No more wondering if you're good enough to be a writer. No more wondering if you have what it takes or if you're wasting your time when you sit down to write. Starting now—with the publication system in front of you—you get to decide for yourself where your writing takes you.

Use this book to build your confidence and writing skills and the stamina it takes to actually be in "the right place at the right time" that is fundamental to luck in the writing business. It's the strategy I followed to land my first publication. I hope you'll join me.

—Mandy

TURN LUCK INTO AN ALLY

▼

No, you can't get around it. There's a certain element of luck or chance each time you submit a story. Will the editor like it? Will it get published? The bad news is—even if you're already a published author—every new submission is a toss-up. That's the part of publication we can't change.

But there's a way around it.

You can't control which way any single submission will go. But the more often you submit, the better your chances are of getting published overall. That's simple statistics.

Oh, that doesn't seem like much of a revelation? Then think of it this way.

Imagine you flip a coin. You want heads, but it comes up tails. Bummer, right? You didn't get what you wanted that time, so you flip the coin again. Maybe it comes up heads. Maybe it comes up tails. But flip that coin a dozen times, and there's only so many times you'll get tails in a row. Eventually, that coin is going to come up the way you want.

Maybe getting published isn't so different.

There's more to publishing, of course. And we'll cover that in the steps you'll find in this book. But if you think about publication as purely a numbers game, getting what you want approaches the inevitable if you just keep flipping that coin and submitting stories.

Even better? With Part One of this publication strategy, your writing will get better each week. That means your chances of publication improve each week, too. (You can't say the same for coin tossing.)

We're not trying to do the impossible here. A path to publication already exists, and people have been traveling it to successful writing careers for awhile now. Why not you?

So write a short story. Submit a short story. Repeat. Because there are only so many times you're going to hear *no* in a row. Next up, how to pull it off.

HOW TO USE THIS BOOK

▼

The goal? Get published this year. The strategy? Play the numbers in a way that's so easy, it's almost unfair. How?

This publication system takes advantage of the supreme predictability of statistics. Since statistics is so predictable, it's actually easy to build our publication system around it.

This publication system accepts what is unchangeable about getting published: not every editor we send a story to this year is going to say yes. Just like every time we toss a coin, we can't be sure we'll get heads. We'll embrace this truth. But we still need a way to tip luck into your favor so well that seeing your name in print this year approaches the inevitable. The basic strategy behind this book is twofold.

One, we need a way to easily and painlessly write our best stories. That way the chances your story sees print improve each time you submit. This is covered in Part One, The Prompts. This part of our strategy is even better than our coin toss example because, unlike tossing coins, your chances of getting published improve with your writing skills each week.

Two, we need a system that maximizes our number of chances for getting published even if we've never published before. That's covered with all the resources you'll find in Part Two, The Submissions. There you'll find your submissions tracker, publication leads, and a cover letter worksheet and template to keep you on track.

Bonus: these resources ensure you always have a new place to send your story. Imagine that just two weeks into this publication strategy you could have two stories and fifty publications to submit to. That's a hundred chances to get published in just two weeks.

Let's look at how the two parts of our publication strategy work together.

THE STRATEGY IN TWO PARTS

▼

01 / THE SHORT STORY PROMPTS

If you follow Ray Bradbury's advice and write a short story each week, you can't help but get better at writing. And although experts say it takes ten thousand hours to become a master at any craft, we don't have to master writing to get our first publication. (Have you seen some of the stories out there in print?) No, we just have to write a story that's good enough. That's easier than you might think if you're writing a story a week.

Why short stories? This is where we see the genius of Bradbury's advice.

I'm not saying it's impossible to get published this year by writing your first novel. But coming from a statistical perspective, it's really unlikely because you'd have to:

- write the 90,000-word novel

- improve your longform story skills like plot, character arcs, setting, and tension so each works in tandem across all 90,000 words

- find beta readers you trust who represent your story's demographic

- wait for those readers to read your novel and send you feedback

- edit those 90,000 words numerous times using multiple points of feedback from various beta readers

- research editors and agents until you find the perfect match

- submit the novel to editors and agents until someone says yes

Looking at it this way, we're better off tackling the short story.

That's because it's important to write a complete story if we want to improve our storytelling skills. That gives you, the writer, an opportunity to practice every important element of story crafting—character, plot, setting, tension, and more—

in the shortest time.

But writing a complete story each week is only possible if the story is short. With a novel, you'd tinker with just one or two story elements in that same week. Maybe you'd improve that particular storytelling skill that week. Maybe you wouldn't.

Bottom line, you need a quicker path to excellence if you want to be published before the year is up.

Besides, it's more satisfying to see your completed works pile up and your writing get better week by week instead of month by month or year by year. And it ensures you have more stories to submit in a shorter amount of time, which means more chances that you'll get one published.

Are you starting to see the genius of this strategy yet?

But what if you don't know what to write about? Part One will spark your writerly imagination with a variety of prompts.

You might be surprised where they take you.

02 / PUBLICATION LEADS + SUBMISSIONS TRACKER

The Landing Your First Publication system is designed to eliminate worries about rejection. We do that by ensuring you always have a next publication to submit your story to and a next story to submit.

Part Two is where you'll find all those publications open to new writers. Try to list at least 5-10 publications for each story. The more publications you find to submit each story to, the greater your chances of publication this year.

You can use your publications list to match publications to each story you write. If you know what each publication is looking for and submit only those stories that match their tastes, it's more likely they'll publish you. Then again, you can also play only to the numbers and submit each story everywhere. More about this and other submissions strategies in Part Two.

The submissions tracker in Part Two will help you keep track of where you've submitted each story and where to send it next. Your submissions tracker makes room for each story you finish and each time you submit. That way you'll never forget whether you already sent a particular story to a particular publication.

And you'll always know where to send it next (unless it gets published!).

Tracking submissions like this will help you avoid duplicate submissions and annoying the editors who might otherwise publish your work. It also makes sure you're sending each story to the maximum number of publications that would potentially be interested in your story. Because, again, more submissions means more chances to get published.

The cover letter worksheet in Part Two will help you figure out what to say in your pitch to the editor. This worksheet and its cover letter template make sure you have everything you need to make a good impression, even if this is your very first submission.

Part One

THE PROMPTS

▼

THERE ARE NO RULES

"If you write one story, it may be bad; if you write a hundred, you have the odds in your favor." —Edgar Rice Buroughs

No matter what you like to write—literary or genre fiction, memoir, poetry, or magazine articles—you're likely to find a prompt here to inspire or surprise a story out of you.

Prompts in this section come in a few different varieties, from villain motivations to the kinds of personal questions that inspire passionate journal entries. But if a question about your personal experiences sparks the backstory for a character instead or a villain motivation opens an angle into that non-fiction article you always wanted to write, let it. There are no rules here.

This isn't high school English class. You won't get a grade for how closely you followed directions or stayed within the lines. This is about inspiring your creativity. Prompting your imagination. Opening you up to the freedom to write. The only thing that matters here is *you* and the stories you get out of your head and onto the page each week.

Don't think you can write an entire short story in a week? Try anyway. Even if some stories take longer to write—which is especially likely with your first few—at the end you'll have a story you didn't have before. And you'll be that much closer to seeing your name in print.

Our goal is publication, not perfection. Each prompt in the pages here is in service to that. Next are a few tips to help you make the most of them.

MORE STORY IN LESS TIME

▼

01 / DON'T DWELL ON ANY ONE STORY

The point behind this system is to write through so many stories that you can't help but improve your writing skills through simple experience. That means no story is precious enough to overlabor or worry over.

Instead, get used to seeing each story as a skills-building exercise.

This may seem counterintuitive when you're trying to write your best work, but a detached mindset when you sit down to write actually gives you the distance you need to become a better writer.

Sentimentality for any one story is actually a hindrance here.

This also frees you from worrying whether any one story is good enough for a particular publication, because the beauty of this strategy is that no one story or publication has the power to make or break your career. There's always a next publication. There's always a next story.

So just follow the steps and let the statistics work for you.

02 / DON'T BE DISCOURAGED BY THE STEAMERS

As Bradbury said, no one can write fifty-two bad stories in a row. But no one can write fifty-two *great* stories in a row either. Some stories will be great. Some may miss the mark.

When you hate that week's story, just move on to the next one. The trend as you write will be an improvement in each batch of new stories every few weeks. And, when the time is right, you can always circle back to a promising story that didn't quite come together.

03 / SUBMIT (ALMOST) EVERY STORY

Even if you thought your story sucked, you might be surprised which ones an editor likes enough to publish. If it isn't a complete steaming pile, submit it anyway. That keeps us tossing the metaphorical coin so that even the crappy stories improve our odds that the next one will make it.

I say submit "almost" every story because you'll know when a story is so flabby that seeing it in print would embarrass more than bring you pride (hey, it's bound to happen).

04 / WRITE WHATEVER POPS INTO YOUR HEAD

You'll notice that each prompt in this book comes with just a little bit of space to write in. This is for a good reason. You want to get down on paper the initial words and images that pop into your mind when you read the prompt. Don't overthink it.

Many new writers feel like they can't write their story down until the words are perfect in their heads, as though committing those imperfect words to paper means they can never change them or (gasp!) that someone will see their draft and think they're a terrible writer. Don't let this be you!

First drafts are meant to be messy. So get those first images or words down on the page, no matter how messy or imperfect they are.

Then, once you know where you're going, find somewhere with enough writing space to continue the story.

05 / USE PROMPTS ACROSS GENRES

We talked a little about this idea already. And it's worth repeating.

We won't explicitly focus on prompts that inspire personal essays, journal entries, or magazine articles. But feel free to use the prompts in that way if and when that works for you.

Did a sci-fi prompt give you an idea for a mystery story set in the real world? Great! Follow where the muse leads.

Remember that this book isn't meant to be a list of rules. Think of it as guidelines you can use in whatever way makes sense to you and your publication goals (even if those goals evolve and change).

If a prompt reminds you of a personal experience you want to write about, embrace it! Whatever works.

Now, let's jump into the prompts.

FICTION PROMPTS

At a chance encounter, his ex-lover tries to prove they've been better off without him.

STORY STARTER

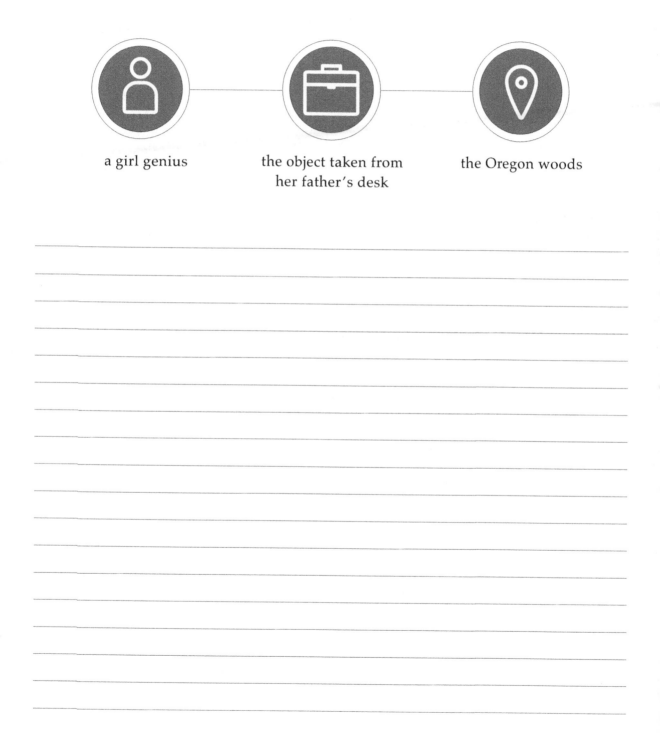

a girl genius

the object taken from her father's desk

the Oregon woods

"You want to name her what?"

_____

_____

_____

_____

_____

_____

"I said I liked it."

_____

_____

_____

_____

_____

_____

"He only ever sees half a thing."

_____

_____

_____

_____

_____

_____

Who you used to be.

You have an idea of where your story plot is going. Let your protagonist choose a different path.

Write a sales page for mud. Make someone want to buy it. Make it expensive.

A conversation between you and your favorite author. Include their body language and what they look, smell, and sound like.

A romance scene between a mop and a broom from the perspective of the vacuum.

You're standing on a cliff with a slingshot in your hand. What happens next?

A time you did a favor for someone, and it backfired.

_____
_____
_____
_____
_____
_____
_____
_____
_____

Describe the best thing about you from the perspective of your house when you come home one night.

_____
_____
_____
_____
_____
_____
_____
_____
_____
_____
_____
_____

Describe your first orgasm.

COMBINE THE ELEMENTS
+ WRITE THE SCENE

1
SOMETHING SHE DIDN'T EXPECT

2
SOMEONE HE COULDN'T HAVE NOTICED

3
THE BYSTANDER IN AN OPEN SPACE

The things
you've carried.

Something you
used to care about.

That time you felt
like a foreigner.

How she changed you.

But I Don't Wanna Wear Pants—An Autobiography

_____

_____

_____

_____

_____

_____

_____

_____

_____

_____

The Narcissist's Guide to Starting a Family

_____

_____

_____

_____

_____

_____

_____

_____

_____

_____

_____

> ## "
>
> *It's none of their business that you have to learn to write. Let them think you were born that way.*
>
> — Ernest Hemingway

A comic book character loses their power and takes an office job.

Name your favorite thing in the world to do or experience. Make that your character's career with one change—they hate it.

Write a story that's told through notes passed in class.

_____

_____

_____

_____

_____

_____

_____

_____

_____

_____

_____

That time you hit on someone, and it turned out better
than you hoped.

_____

_____

_____

_____

_____

_____

_____

_____

_____

_____

_____

WRITE YOUR GREATEST SECRET AS FICTION. DON'T TELL ANYONE IT'S TRUE.

Write a scene from the Iliad set in modern-day America. Write it in less than 2000 words.

The Beginner's Guide to God-Speaking

_____
_____
_____
_____
_____
_____
_____

How to Raise an Asshole

_____
_____
_____
_____
_____
_____
_____

The Homeless Girl's Guide to Life

_____
_____
_____
_____
_____
_____
_____

The first time you ate your favorite dish (even if you don't remember it).

A dialogue scene of the conversation you wish you'd never had.

Your most embarassing moment from a bystander's perspective.

IF YOU WERE A GOD, WHAT WOULD YOU BE GOD OF? WHAT WOULD YOUR DAILY LIFE BE LIKE?

What dying feels like.

When the villain was
wrongly accused.

The one who falls
in love too soon.

Where seven
roads meet.

Two versions of you argue over giving up a bad habit. Write it as a dialogue scene. One of you wins.

_____

_____

_____

_____

_____

_____

_____

_____

_____

_____

If you could be guaranteed fame for writing any story, what would the story be about?

_____

_____

_____

_____

_____

_____

_____

_____

_____

_____

_____

YOU WAKE UP INSIDE
THE COLD STORAGE OF
A RESTAURANT WITH
NO MEMORY OF HOW
YOU GOT THERE.

Tell a character in a horror movie how to survive. Write it like a how-to blog post.

STORY STARTER

a sous-chef with
the worst luck

a dull kitchen knife

a taco truck next to
an overflowing lake

Something you weren't
supposed to see.

"What did you do
after you killed him?"

"Ma'am, please
relinquish the bag."

A homeless man
wins the lottery.

You find a diary in a bus station that mentions a large sum of cash buried in a trailer park outside Guthrie. You think you can piece together the clues to find out where it is.

"You always talk to me like I insulted your mama."

_____
_____
_____
_____
_____
_____
_____
_____
_____

They find something valuable inside the trick drawer of an estate
sale purchase.

_____
_____
_____
_____
_____
_____
_____
_____
_____
_____
_____

"

Get it down. Take chances.
It may be bad, but it's
the only way you can do
anything really good.

— William Faulkner —

You're waiting at the bus stop when you meet the power couple that changes your life.

Look at yourself in the mirror. Write about that person as though you've never seen them before.

His elevator shuts down on the way to the interview—just when his IBS starts to act up.

"If you hit that button even half a second too late, we all die."

The new hire decides to blow the whistle on his company two days into the job.

That time someone made you feel bad for wanting to be a writer.
Tell them why their opinion was dumb.

_____
_____
_____
_____
_____
_____
_____
_____
_____
_____
_____
_____
_____
_____
_____
_____
_____
_____
_____
_____
_____
_____
_____
_____
_____

A terrible life experience which you turned out better for.

_____

_____

_____

_____

_____

_____

A letter to your child self.

_____

_____

_____

_____

_____

_____

The smell of your grandmother's home.

_____

_____

_____

_____

_____

_____

They watch shows together most nights to pretend they still have things in common. Then the power dies.

ALL SHE EVER WANTED
WAS SOMEONE WHO
WOULD TAKE CONTROL.
SHE THINKS SHE'S FINALLY
FOUND HIM, UNTIL HE
SHOWS A WEAKNESS.

A little girl finds a bag of gold buried in her backyard. What does she do with it?

_____

_____

_____

_____

_____

_____

_____

_____

_____

_____

_____

Describe your first memory. Use all five senses.

_____

_____

_____

_____

_____

_____

_____

_____

_____

_____

_____

_____

"You look at me like you know me. But I don't know you."

"With an attitude like that, friend, you won't soon greet a pair of open legs."

"Pretty girls have more fun," her mother told her. "But pretty can be dangerous."

Would you rather be an astronaut or a CEO? Why?

"MEAN FACE, TINY WAIST. WHO WOULDN'T BE INTO HER?"

He could do anything in this kind of weather.

_____

_____

_____

_____

_____

_____

_____

"People always say I surprise them."

_____

_____

_____

_____

_____

_____

_____

You don't have to.

_____

_____

_____

_____

_____

_____

_____

"You may not be worth the effort of full-on revenge. But I wouldn't advise you to scurry past when I have a free boot."

A woman tries to convince another woman of something while they fix a broken window on a house.

Describe something you wanted desperately as a child. Write a scene in which you got it, and it disappoints.

How you knew it was a lie.

The one question you'd ask an animal if it could answer in your native language. And what the animal would say.

An elderly retired superhero creates his bio on a matchmaking website.

_____

_____

_____

_____

_____

_____

_____

_____

_____

_____

You're the assistant manager at a fast food joint whose job it is to sort through the customer feedback tickets. You discover a plea for help stamped 2:45 every day. It's 2:43.

_____

_____

_____

_____

_____

_____

_____

_____

_____

_____

_____

A shy college kid enlists a phobia psychiatrist to help him talk to girls.

"

*This is how you do it:
you sit down at the
keyboard and you put one
word after another until
it's done. It's that easy,
and that hard.*

Neil Gaiman

She found it buried inside a bag of fertilizer from the home
improvement store.

"MOM, COME GET ME. I FOUND SOMETHING IN THE TRUNK OF DAD'S CAR."

The elderly neighbor you once nursed back to health names you his heir upon his death.

A woman finds out she's pregnant two months after her husband dies.

STORY STARTER

a radicalized government agent — a box of industrial lightbulbs — a warehouse in a foreign country

_____

_____

_____

_____

_____

_____

_____

_____

_____

_____

_____

_____

_____

_____

_____

_____

_____

"That wasn't part of the deal."

A day in the life of a cockroach.

"I swear. I left it right here."

A pitbull adjusts to his new place in the family when his owners
bring home their firstborn.

An Ed McMahon look-alike runs a scam in a senior home.

"When this is over, you'll
wish we'd never met."

An emotional scene
featuring an acquaintance.

Something important that
turned out to be untrue.

"You're just saying that
because you don't know..."

While sweeping online prostitution ads, a vice officer finds an account with a picture of her sister-in-law.

A woman undergoes hypnosis to cure her nicotine addiction only to wake up every morning outside the cigarette store with no memory of how she got there.

A boy finds a secret door in the storage room of his grandparents' house.

_____

_____

_____

_____

_____

_____

_____

_____

_____

Have a conversation with your character. Ask him why he's giving you so much trouble.

_____

_____

_____

_____

_____

_____

_____

_____

_____

_____

_____

_____

COMBINE THE ELEMENTS
+ WRITE THE SCENE

1
A NAIVE OFFICE WORKER
▼

2
A DEAD PERSON'S SOCIAL MEDIA ACCOUNT
▼

3
AN OLD RECIPE WITH A DANGEROUS INGREDIENT
▼

After buying their dream home, a family discovers that the electrical transmission tower near their property exacerbates their daughter's disease, and they can't afford to move.

_____

_____

_____

_____

_____

_____

_____

_____

_____

_____

_____

_____

_____

_____

_____

_____

_____

_____

_____

_____

_____

_____

_____

All drugs are legalized.

And then he left.

A flower delivery and
an unpleasant surprise.

You discover a skeleton
during a home renovation.

"No way is that coming in here."

"

One day I will find
the right words, and
they will be simple.

Jack Kerouac

Turns out it was just one more way to die.

_____

_____

_____

_____

_____

_____

_____

"I think it's gone."

_____

_____

_____

_____

_____

_____

The thing he couldn't tell her.

_____

_____

_____

_____

_____

_____

What are the top three characteristics you look for in a romantic partner? Write a villain who demonstrates those qualities.

"SHE'S A MATCHSTICK WOMAN IN A TINDER WORLD."

It's time.

"I don't think he knows what he's eating."

"He said it would be here, but I didn't believe him."

_____

_____

_____

_____

_____

_____

_____

_____

It came out of the water.

_____

_____

_____

_____

_____

_____

_____

_____

_____

STORY STARTER

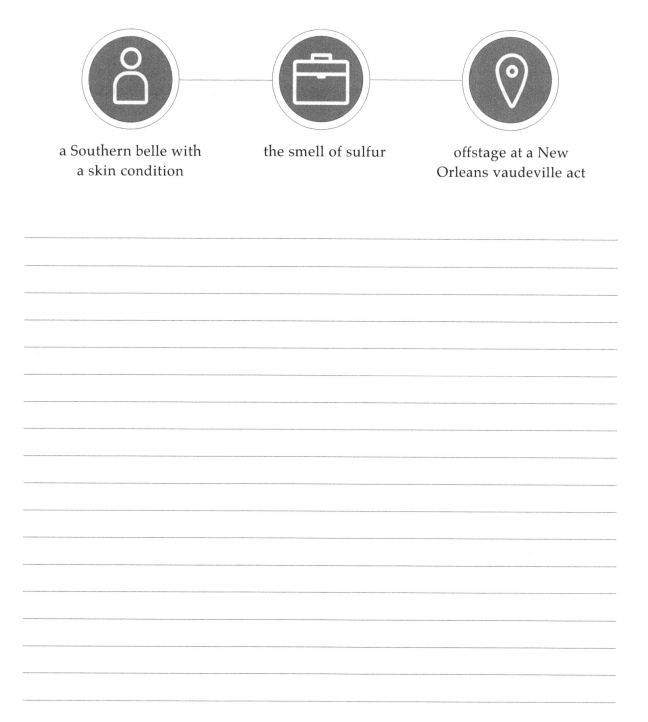

a Southern belle with a skin condition

the smell of sulfur

offstage at a New Orleans vaudeville act

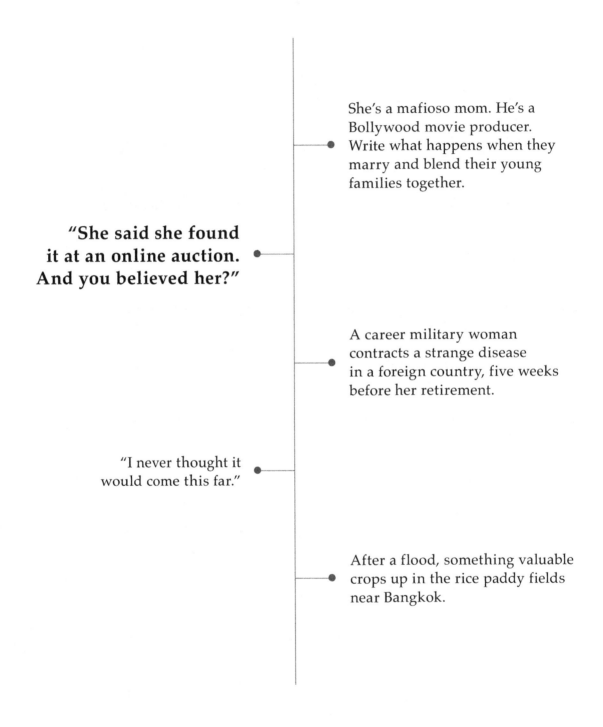

She's a mafioso mom. He's a
Bollywood movie producer.
Write what happens when they
marry and blend their young
families together.

**"She said she found
it at an online auction.
And you believed her?"**

A career military woman
contracts a strange disease
in a foreign country, five weeks
before her retirement.

"I never thought it
would come this far."

After a flood, something valuable
crops up in the rice paddy fields
near Bangkok.

An art dealer finds the thing he's been searching for in the bathroom of a cheap motel.

"You see that couple down there with the box of flowers? They aren't who they say they are."

Three families face a crisis at a mountain resort.

_____

_____

_____

_____

_____

_____

_____

And who could blame her?

_____

_____

_____

_____

_____

_____

_____

"Either you finish this now, or you get hauled in."

_____

_____

_____

_____

_____

_____

_____

Everything is temporary.

"I know it looks the
same, but it's not."

"I'll tell you next
time I see you."

Maybe it was time
to meet in real life.

The florist gripped that baby's breath in a white-knuckled fist.

_____

_____

_____

_____

_____

_____

_____

_____

_____

_____

The grumpy old man next door runs over your cat and then
asks for a favor.

_____

_____

_____

_____

_____

_____

_____

_____

_____

_____

_____

_____

A DESPERATE, SINGLE MOTHER MEETS EXACTLY THE PERSON SHE NEEDS WHEN SHE ROBS A LOCAL COFFEE SHOP.

An old slave tells the children around a campfire what it was like
when he ruled the world.

"

And by the way, everything in life is writable about if you have the outgoing guts to do it, and the imagination to improvise. The worst enemy to creativity is self-doubt.

— Sylvia Plath

The signs along the riverbank said, "Danger. Do not enter." But the river was dry.

"Of course Heaven is real. And I can take you there for $73.99."

———————————————
———————————————
———————————————
———————————————
———————————————
———————————————
———————————————
———————————————
———————————————
———————————————
———————————————

Twin brothers, separated at birth and reunited at 34, switch lives for a year.

———————————————
———————————————
———————————————
———————————————
———————————————
———————————————
———————————————
———————————————
———————————————
———————————————
———————————————
———————————————

STORY STARTER

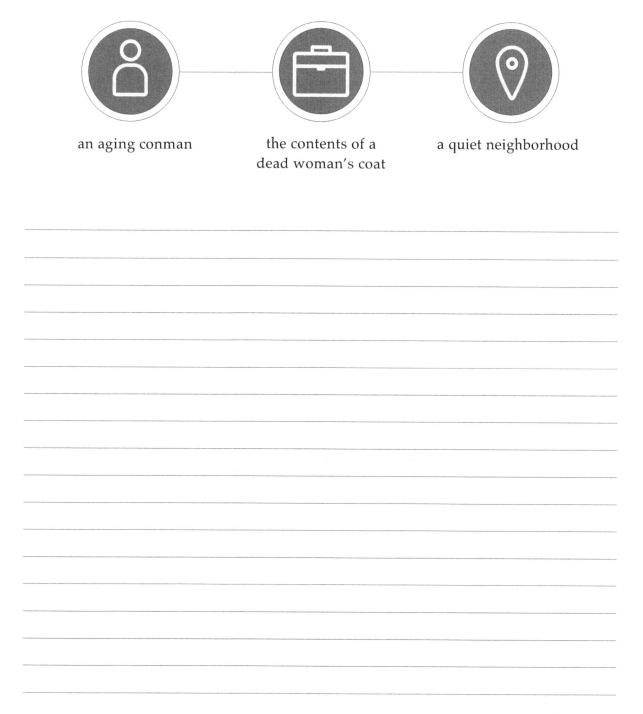

an aging conman

the contents of a dead woman's coat

a quiet neighborhood

He's calm on the surface, but the current runs deep.

_____

_____

_____

_____

_____

_____

They call him Johnny Lightfingers.

_____

_____

_____

_____

_____

_____

"What if it's still there when we get back?"

_____

_____

_____

_____

_____

_____

A recent graduate lands his dream job in politics only to be welcomed by a nightmare administration.

It was in his eyes.

"Watch this."

✛

"Look out!"

She played it on loop.

A woman is relieved when a man steals her purse in the park.

An unlikely romance comes out of a narrowly avoided tragedy.

_____

_____

_____

_____

_____

_____

_____

_____

_____

_____

He never password protected his wireless printer. One day a
neighbor prints something he never wanted to see.

_____

_____

_____

_____

_____

_____

_____

_____

_____

_____

A woman on the run wins an extravagant sum at a slot machine.
Her enemy sees the story on the nightly news.

"Onward and tallyho and all that."

No pressure. It's just the whole country watching.

_____

_____

_____

_____

_____

_____

_____

_____

_____

_____

_____

_____

_____

_____

_____

_____

_____

_____

_____

_____

_____

_____

_____

A TV HOST HAS AN ON-AIR MELTDOWN.

"It's not my fault! I told her to stand still!"

_____
_____
_____
_____
_____
_____
_____
_____
_____
_____

A taboo look becomes a global fashion trend.

_____
_____
_____
_____
_____
_____
_____
_____
_____
_____
_____

A famous blogger goes missing after publishing a cryptic post.

A dinner party goes wrong when the hosts reveal a terrible secret.

COMBINE THE ELEMENTS
+ WRITE THE SCENE

1
A HIGH-DEMAND JOB
▼

2
A CHARITY COMPETITION
▼

3
A BROKEN DOWN MUSCLE CAR
▼

The lie you've been telling yourself.

What you've been searching for.

✖

"Time's up."

"You didn't see this coming?"

"It was hard to accept that my judgement about you could be so wrong."

A Good Samaritan helps someone in need and winds up in legal trouble.

STORY STARTER

an antiques
broker with a secret

a knock-off of
high value

the pristine cellar of
an old woman's farm

A freestyle kissing competition.

_____
_____
_____
_____
_____
_____

"Look how fancy you are."

_____
_____
_____
_____
_____
_____

"Before you go, a warning."

_____
_____
_____
_____
_____
_____

A man refuses to check out of his hotel when his career and home life spin out of control.

"If you aren't making a mess, you aren't doing it right."

"So what's it like to be the most hated person in the office?"

_____

_____

_____

_____

_____

_____

_____

_____

_____

_____

A valet driver takes a customer's car for a joy ride and finds
something life-changing under the driver seat.

_____

_____

_____

_____

_____

_____

_____

_____

_____

_____

_____

"You could feed a million starving people on a single fish, and someone would still complain."

"It can't be erupting if there's still ice on the ridge. Right?"

A troubled family wins an all-expenses paid trip abroad and ends up finding something they needed even more.

_____

_____

_____

_____

_____

_____

_____

_____

_____

_____

_____

_____

_____

_____

_____

_____

_____

_____

_____

_____

_____

_____

_____

_____

_____

_____

A dog trainer specializing in positive reinforcement is recruited to train prison inmates in impulse control.

"

The scariest moment is always just before you start.

Stephen King

"Knock again."

_____

The marksman knelt down in the dust.

_____

Tallahassee Mitchell never had it so good.

"It's just not gonna happen."

STORY STARTER

a sculptor with
big ambition

a material of
little value

an impoverished
neighborhood

He tied his shoes, dusted himself off, and stepped up to the ledge.

It just wasn't
exciting anymore.

They said it would
be harder than this.

"Want to take a
ride on my camel?"

"I swear he's
not a bad person."

Turns out she was right.

"You promised you wouldn't get mad."

A photographer witnesses a crime through the lens of his camera while on a helicopter aerial shoot.

A drug trafficker's son tries desperately to give away ten million dollars of guilt money, but everyone thinks he's just a scammer.

Because time is unkind.

_____

_____

_____

_____

_____

_____

_____

"Close your eyes."

_____

_____

_____

_____

_____

_____

_____

"No one he could attract is someone we want around."

_____

_____

_____

_____

_____

_____

_____

She should have known better than to answer a call from an
unrecognized number.

"Maybe just one more time."

_____

_____

_____

_____

_____

_____

_____

_____

_____

_____

_____

_____

_____

_____

_____

_____

_____

_____

_____

_____

_____

_____

_____

_____

The last thing he remembers is popping the hood of the stranger's car.

_____

_____

_____

_____

_____

_____

_____

_____

_____

In her many fantasies of this moment, the one-way ticket never cost so much.

_____

_____

_____

_____

_____

_____

_____

_____

_____

_____

A man calls his online retailer about the empty box he received by mail. The rep: "Sir, you need to leave your house right now."

SCIENCE FICTION
PROMPTS

The polar magnets reverse, frying all electronics on Earth. Write what happens in the months it takes to replace them.

_____

_____

_____

_____

_____

_____

_____

_____

_____

After a scientist disproves the theory behind faster-than-light travel, it suddenly stops working.

_____

_____

_____

_____

_____

_____

_____

_____

_____

_____

_____

_____

Raznel Corp offers its
deepest condolences.

First contact, from
the alien's POV.

The daily routine of an old
man, 200 years from now.

A depressed AI
program dies by suicide.

A scientist discovers why God can't communicate with humans.

A man falls asleep and wakes up on a different
planet as a different species.

A WOMAN SENDS DAILY LETTERS TO THE ARCHIVES OF A COLONIZATION SHIP WHERE HER CHILDREN RIDE IN STASIS.

While testing a new mood inhibitor lamp in Alaska's dark season for a pharmaceutical company, a group of subjects begin to exhibit dangerous psychological abnormalities.

"Drink this. You'll live. But you'll be different."

_____

_____

_____

_____

_____

_____

_____

_____

_____

A recent discovery proves that, at one point, all planets in our solar system were populated with life.

_____

_____

_____

_____

_____

_____

_____

_____

_____

_____

_____

An orphan boy finds he can pick up radio signals with his mind.

"You're not seriously
out of air credits already?"

A dog show for genetically
engineered breeds.

Romeo & Juliet
as a space opera.

"Hello again,
Agent Marshall."

He falls in love with the live-in android purchased to serve him.

_____

_____

_____

_____

_____

_____

_____

_____

_____

_____

Upgrade the graphics card in your eyes for better
than 20/20 vision.

_____

_____

_____

_____

_____

_____

_____

_____

_____

_____

_____

_____

A robotics engineer takes advantage of a refugee crisis to avert a catastrophe.

Due to a mechanical failure, a delivery drone drops a heavy
shipment on a busy commuter crowd below.

_____

_____

_____

_____

_____

_____

_____

_____

_____

_____

_____

A book hoarder in a digital information society refuses to seek help
for his addiction.

_____

_____

_____

_____

_____

_____

_____

_____

_____

_____

_____

_____

A farmers market booth
of interplanetary delicacies.

Five ways your life is easier
with self-driving cars.

The invention
you wish was real.

The path to eternal life
through voluntary death.

During a global food shortage, an advertising agency is hired to change the country's mind about bugs as a primary protein source.

"If it has to be my last day on Earth, I'm glad I get to spend it with you."

A furniture maker is out of work when the town installs a
community 3D printing machine.

_____

_____

_____

_____

_____

_____

_____

_____

_____

_____

A down-and-out mechanic sabotages offworlders' spacecrafts to
make extra cash.

_____

_____

_____

_____

_____

_____

_____

_____

_____

_____

_____

So much had changed in 300 years, and she wasn't glad to be back.

It's what they call star power.

"

I write to give myself strength. I write to be the characters that I am not. I write to explore all the things I'm afraid of.

Joss Whedon

AFTER GROWING UP IN VIRTUAL REALITY, FIVE ORPHAN CHILDREN EXPERIENCE THE REAL WORLD FOR THE FIRST TIME.

A neuroscientist claims she can "cure" fundamentalist thinking.

A wildlife preserve for interplanetary endangered species is
threatened with mass extinction.

An intelligent, subterranean Earth species expands into human territory after a meteor strike causes a nuclear winter.

Refugees from a war-torn planet step off their ship only to find a new enemy.

An attempt to make the predatory wildlife on a new planet more docile backfires.

"Nobody that knows anything is
gonna talk to the Shree."

Gene repair in twenty-five
minutes, or it's free!

No ridge. No tail.
No service.

"I'm sorry. He never
said he was human."

"I don't know, man. The S.S. Titanic is an inauspicous name for an Earth orbit cruise ship."

_____

_____

_____

_____

_____

_____

_____

_____

_____

Bone density readings indicate they were born on this planet.

_____

_____

_____

_____

_____

_____

_____

_____

_____

_____

Sources say the battery on her nutrition pack died at 21:05.

_____
_____
_____
_____
_____
_____
_____
_____
_____
_____

"You want I should knock out their light drive?"

_____
_____
_____
_____
_____
_____
_____
_____
_____
_____
_____

An ailing elderly couple depends on androids to meet
their daily needs.

_____

_____

_____

_____

_____

_____

_____

_____

_____

_____

The sign read, "No Earthers permitted within 100 meters."

_____

_____

_____

_____

_____

_____

_____

_____

_____

_____

_____

_____

"COME ON, BABY. SHE WAS JUST AN ANDROID."

A mining colony faces civil war when an unexpected ion storm threatens to cut off food and medical shipments from their sponsor planet.

But for the crew of SB221, nuclear fallout was just the beginning.

_____

_____

_____

_____

_____

_____

_____

_____

_____

_____

"Listen, mister. If you don't have the credits, you're gonna have to give back the Taque cube."

_____

_____

_____

_____

_____

_____

_____

_____

_____

_____

Discounts only for senior members aged 251 and older.

"DON'T LOOK SO GRIM. IT'S JUST THE END OF THE WORLD."

To test a new vaccine, a corporation hides it inside personal care products distributed in a third world country. Write from the perspective of a suspicious humanitarian aid worker when a strange virus breaks out.

Spacewalks, €25.

Last ship to the Belt at 06:36.

"Houston, tell my wife I didn't suffer."

"I don't make the rules, kid. If you want off this rock, this is the only way."

After a two hundred light-year trip to an uninhabited planet, a group of settlers disembarks to find an alien city already erected. It's perfectly preserved, but abandoned.

"I found his transporter hovering over Qinong Hill with its axles up."

"If he's the spy, then Mars already has the codes."

_____

_____

_____

_____

_____

_____

_____

_____

_____

Overwhelmed with student debt, a xenobiology geneticist creates
exotic hybrid animal species to sell on the black market.

_____

_____

_____

_____

_____

_____

_____

_____

_____

_____

_____

"

Finish what you start. Keep submitting until it sells.

Robert Heinlein

A drought on Earth shifts political power to Mars.

_____
_____
_____
_____
_____
_____
_____

They wouldn't be home for another 800 years.

_____
_____
_____
_____
_____
_____
_____

His home planet was awash in volcanic ash.

_____
_____
_____
_____
_____
_____
_____

What happens in tyrant-controlled countries when a new internet—one that's lightning fast and can't be blocked—makes censorship impossible?

"Nah, we ain't allowed. Prophet says playing with outmoon tech turns you into a girl."

"We both knew
the air wasn't free."

Forget bad experiences
with MemWipe™ 2.0.

We're on Sphere One time
the second we hit atmo.

"This was your brain
before the upgrade."

In the year 7523, two archaeologists break ground on a previously undiscovered ruin. The first artifact they uncover is a sign that reads, Arbeit Macht Frei.

_____

_____

_____

_____

_____

_____

_____

_____

_____

"She calls it the edge of the universe. But it's just quadrant three."

_____

_____

_____

_____

_____

_____

_____

_____

_____

_____

_____

Customs confiscates a phoney FTL drive only to discover it works.

_____
_____
_____
_____
_____
_____
_____
_____
_____
_____

"I don't care if he isn't human, Daddy. I love him."

_____
_____
_____
_____
_____
_____
_____
_____
_____
_____
_____

100 years ago, her family created the first interstellar communication device. She puts it up for auction when she falls on hard times.

"But everyone who goes to Ganna 4 comes back pregnant."

A family with special abilities performs across the globe while secretly using their gifts for an underground purpose.

_____

_____

_____

_____

_____

_____

_____

_____

_____

A travel writer explores the 12 Sisters, a series of man-made planets along the galactic rim.

_____

_____

_____

_____

_____

_____

_____

_____

_____

_____

LEADERS OF A THIRD WORLD COUNTRY USE NEW MEDICAL TECHNOLOGY TO ELIMINATE CIVIL UNREST. THE TECHNOLOGY? A DEVICE ORIGINALLY INVENTED TO CURE DRUG ADDICTS AND THE MENTALLY ILL BY REWIRING THEIR BRAINS.

After 50 years of use, a teleportation system is discovered to not actually transport matter but to replicate it at a new location, destroying the original.

When every moment is recorded and searchable online, personal privacy becomes an antiquated concept. What's it like to live in a culture that no longer values or expects privacy?

VILLAINS + ANTI-HEROES

PROMPTS FOR THE LESS NOBLE MOTIVATIONS

He does it for the LOLs.

A necrophiliac undertaker.

A reformed villain's
victim back for revenge.

The rebel against authority
under an immoral parent.

Left for dead and raised in horror foster care, a teen girl finds out her parents are alive, well, and wealthy.

His mother didn't want him to leave her side, so she taught him all women are suspect.

He'll stop at nothing to hide the past that would damage his pristine reputation.

_____

_____

_____

_____

_____

_____

_____

_____

_____

_____

Her kingdom was stolen. She wants it back.

_____

_____

_____

_____

_____

_____

_____

_____

_____

_____

_____

She fell in with a bad employer. Now she's stuck carrying out the destructive duties or risks losing her family's only source of income.

A YOUNG, NATURAL
LEADER FROM AN
IMPOVERISHED
BACKGROUND USES
STREET METHODS TO
BUILD A STABLE AND
PEACEFUL COMMUNITY.

A peacekeeper from a minority background inflicts cruelty on his community to avoid accusations of favoritism.

A beleaguered superhero gives up and joins the other side when the people are swayed by propaganda.

In a culture that demands men marry their brother's widow, a dangerous man falls in love with her while his brother still lives.

She'll protect her children no matter the cost and no matter what her children do.

She is the paragon of virtue in a society that requires abstinence before marriage. He'll stop at nothing to bring her low enough to conquer.

The illegitimate son of a corporate tycoon acts as the company
enforcer to gain his father's love and attention.

_____

_____

_____

_____

_____

_____

_____

_____

_____

_____

_____

_____

_____

_____

_____

_____

_____

_____

_____

_____

_____

_____

A don juan refuses to believe he has HIV and continues his
unprotected exploits.

A supreme strategist decides to take legal but devastating revenges
on the company that fired him.

A pedophile goes into teaching to be close to kids.

A psychiatrist manipulates patients into pulling heists.

The sociopath who takes extreme risks for the rush.

A hedonist becomes a priest to escape his impoverished roots and hides his hypocrisy behind a pious facade.

He believes the only way to start a fresh, new world is to raze the existing one to the ground.

A professor who fears he is becoming obsolete begins to undermine his student's efforts.

_____

_____

_____

_____

_____

_____

_____

_____

_____

_____

_____

_____

_____

_____

_____

_____

_____

_____

_____

_____

_____

_____

_____

An accountant embezzles money to pay for her sick child's medical bills.

The cowardly moralist
with a taste for power.

The minister who believes
he's God's punishing hand.

He'll teach women
for rejecting him.

He destroys everything
he loves to preserve it.

A lawman takes bribes, so his corrupt peers won't turn against him.

He lost his lover and now wants every other couple to
suffer the same.

This second-in-command resents his role and secretly undermines
his boss's every effort.

_____

_____

_____

_____

_____

_____

_____

_____

_____

_____

An addict who will do anything for a score betrays the protagonist
when she needs him most.

_____

_____

_____

_____

_____

_____

_____

_____

_____

_____

_____

You're a psychopath. Observe the lives of those around you. What do you see? What do everyday activities and human interactions look like to you?

HE'S AFRAID HIS
DAUGHTER WILL
OUTGROW HIM,
SO HE REFUSES TO
LET HER GO TO
THE SCHOOL THAT
WILL FULFILL
HER POTENTIAL.

A corporate leader, under pressure to investors, destroys an eco-system to increase short-term profits.

_____

_____

_____

_____

_____

_____

_____

_____

_____

_____

They didn't recognize his genius in the interview, so he orchestrates a hostile takeover of their company.

_____

_____

_____

_____

_____

_____

_____

_____

_____

_____

This entrepreneur at a small startup hates losing free labor, so he gives his interns poor references when potential new employers call.

_____

_____

_____

_____

_____

_____

_____

_____

_____

_____

_____

_____

_____

_____

_____

_____

_____

_____

_____

_____

_____

_____

_____

_____

_____

_____

A computer science dropout wants to prove he's smarter than everyone else by hacking and destroying their systems.

_____

_____

_____

_____

_____

_____

_____

_____

_____

He believes nothing matters, so he drifts from one destructive action to the next.

_____

_____

_____

_____

_____

_____

_____

_____

_____

_____

"

If there's a book that you want to read, but it hasn't been written yet, then you must write it.

Toni Morrison

The social climber who
believes his ascension is fated.

A short man who eats tall
women to gain their stature.

The resentful robin hood
enslaved to a billionaire.

A mid-level bureaucrat working
for a corrupt government.

"They say the ends don't justify the means. But this is too important."

SIDEKICKS + SIDE CHARACTERS

REASONS FOR THEM TO STICK AROUND

It's his job.

They're married.

He has nowhere else to go.

She owes the hero something.

He wants to be famous.

_____

_____

_____

_____

_____

_____

_____

_____

_____

She wants a life of adventure.

_____

_____

_____

_____

_____

_____

_____

_____

_____

_____

He secretly runs a lucrative Instagram account featuring
the hero's exploits.

To undermine the hero's efforts, he pretends to be her friend.

He wanted to get close enough to the hero to overthrow him, but he fell in love instead.

_____

_____

_____

_____

_____

_____

_____

_____

_____

_____

_____

_____

_____

_____

_____

_____

_____

_____

_____

_____

_____

_____

_____

_____

_____

She hopes it will lead to her freedom.

_____

_____

_____

_____

_____

_____

In the hopes he'll earn the hero's respect.

_____

_____

_____

_____

_____

_____

She wants to reform the anti-hero.

_____

_____

_____

_____

_____

_____

He manipulates the hero's power to achieve his private aims.

SHE WANTS TO
BE A SUPERHERO
SOMEDAY. FOR
NOW, SHE INTERNS
FOR ONE.

He feels he must protect the hero.

She's the hero's slave.

The hero couldn't manage without him.

"Sometimes a person sticks around 'cause it's all he's ever known.
Or maybe I'm just telling myself that."

_____

_____

_____

_____

_____

_____

_____

_____

_____

_____

_____

_____

_____

_____

_____

_____

_____

_____

_____

_____

_____

_____

_____

Part Two

_____

THE SUBMISSIONS

YOUR PUBLICATION RESOURCES

submissions tracker, cover letter template, worksheet

So, your story's all set. It's written, edited, made the rounds for feedback, and you've polished it up. You've got your tough skin zipped up tight in anticipation of your first rejection letter. You sure? Okay, good for you! You're ready to submit your story.

For this publication strategy to work, the next thing you'll need is places to submit your story. A lot of them.

Remember our publication dreams only approach the inevitable if we toss that proverbial coin as many times as it takes. That means submitting as many of our stories to as many publications as possible. And that means lots of stories. And lots of publications.

The resources in this section have you covered.

Here you'll find your submissions tracker, where to find publications that are looking for stories, a cover letter worksheet and template to help you write that all-important pitch. You'll also find how best to match the right publication to your story, so each has the maximum chance of seeing print.

First up? Those publication leads.

WHERE TO SUBMIT STORIES

▼

Has someone told you the short story market isn't what it used to be?

Don't let the news discourage you. From online and literary magazines to short story anthologies—there are plenty of publications looking for short stories, articles, and personal essays. So many, actually, that it would be impossible to list them all here. So we're not going to try.

Instead, I'll point you toward the great resources that frequently update their short story publications lists. Some of these resources go in-depth with information like acceptance and payment rates. Some give you just enough information to get you started, so research them and their reputations to make sure they're a good fit for you and your story.

Here are the best (and mostly free) ways to find those publications.

01 / ONLINE SEARCH ENGINES

Here's an easy place to start if you're brand new to submitting work. A simple online search for "where to submit short stories" will get you started with hundreds of publication leads. You'll find all the usual suspects from newsstands like *Ploughshares*, *The New Yorker*, and *American Short Stories*. A few of them you won't have heard of. That's okay as long as you do your research to make sure they match your goals.

02 / THE REVIEW REVIEW

Looking to publish literary fiction? The Review Review is your go-to database of free-to-browse literary magazines accepting submissions. Search their database in alphabetical order or use the search function to filter magazines by genre, how much they pay, how soon they respond, and when they accept submissions.

The Review Review also offers a classifieds section with calls for submissions, which means a ready list of publications you can be sure are accepting submissions right now. Their reviews offer insight into what each publication is looking for. Use those guidelines for inspiration or to know which of your stories match.

Find them at: http://www.thereviewreview.net/magazines

03 / HEY PUBLISHER

Another online database of publications that's free to use, Hey Publisher covers publications ranging from literary to general interest and everything in between. Test your writerly range with this database of fiction and poetry, articles, book reviews, memoirs, and even essays.

Find them at: https://www.heypublisher.com/publishers/search

04 / THE GRINDER

The Grinder is a publication database and submissions tracker from Diabolical Plots, a science fiction and fantasy magazine. But their publication database covers more than just sci-fi and fantasy. They've collected over five thousand publications ranging from literary to crime fiction. And you can filter your results by story length, pay rates, and average response times. The database is free to search and offers a submissions tracker.

Find them at: https://thegrinder.diabolicalplots.com

05 / SFWA MARKET REPORT

If your writing focus is mainly speculative fiction, try the Science Fiction Writers of America's monthly market report for science fiction and fantasy markets. This report covers new markets, contest openings, and theme changes for their publication leads. You'll have to check back monthly, but that's just because they update so often.

Find them at: http://www.sfwa.org/tag/market-report/

06 / WRITER'S MARKET

This is the motherlode of writing market leads, hence the (small) price tag.

The investment you'll make in a copy of this tome is more than worth it for the sheer number of leads and the depth of information available for each listed publication. F+W publishes it annually, so it's always up to date. It covers publications across a range of genres, editors, and agents looking for new authors. Purchasing a hard copy of the book gives you access to their searchable directory of publications, where you can filter by pay rates and other features.

But if you're reluctant to shell out the cash for a personal copy, many libraries and writing groups carry a copy for members to borrow.

Find it at: https://www.writersdigestshop.com

07 / NEWSSTANDS

What's great about the magazines you'll find on newsstands is that they pay. What's not so great about the magazines you'll find on newsstands is that everyone wants to publish in them, making them tough to break into.

Does that mean you shouldn't submit your work to one as a new writer? Not necessarily.

The New Yorker rarely publishes new writers. But *American Short Stories* and *Tin House* do. Both look specifically for emerging writers or hold contests where emerging writers have frequently placed.

But don't be surprised if your first publication comes from somewhere else. This is why it pays to submit relentlessly to multiple publications and to track those submissions in your submissions tracker. Publications with high competition may offer lower chances of publication. But why not submit to them anyway? We're playing the numbers here.

08 / WHATEVER YOU'RE READING

Don't overlook the power of magazine articles or the personal essay. Just because a story happens to be true, doesn't mean you won't use elements of fiction storytelling to write your tale. And many publications that don't publish short fiction will publish a personal essay.

Who publishes personal essays? Many of the publications you're reading right now, both online and off. Flip through their pages or browse their archives for examples of personal essays they've published before to see if yours might be a good fit. Then pitch it to the editor using the cover letter worksheet and template ahead.

Quick Tip: List Potential Publications Based on Your Goals

Choose the submission strategy best suited to your publication goals.

For example, are you looking for the quickest route to publication? Submit to places with the quickest response times like *Black Mirror*, *Flash*, *New Pop Lit*, and *Entropy*.

Care more about prestige, even if it means a six to twelve month wait between each submission? Start each round with top-tier publications like *The New Yorker*, *Plough Shares*, *Tin House*, and *Granta*.

Maybe getting paid for your work is what makes you feel most like a professional author? Then places like *AGNI*, *Boulevard*, *Carve*, and *Vestal Review* are for you.

Databases in this section, like The Review Review, can filter publications by how much they pay and how long they take to respond to submissions. So use the filters to find the publications most suited to your goals. You can always change up your strategy later.

TO MATCH PUBLICATIONS—OR NOT?

Conventional wisdom says that if you want to pitch your story to a publication, first read everything they've published. Saturate yourself in their style, tone, and preferred POV. Understand the publication inside and out, so you know if they're likely to accept or reject your submission before you send it.

This seems like good advice on the surface. It makes us feel like we have some control in what is ultimately a hit and miss process. And it appeals to the part of us that wants desperately to avoid rejection. And, hey, maybe it will help you avoid a few rejections. But you know what else helps you avoid rejection? Never submitting at all.

Which is a good reminder that the ultimate goal in this process isn't to avoid rejection. The ultimate goal is to get published. What does it matter if you avoid a few rejections here and there when you'll inevitably rack up twenty times more than the few you avoid? Was all that time and energy worth it?

There are simply too many publications out there for any one person to understand the preferences at each. There are too many editors and slush pile readers with their own particular tastes, each with a different take on your story depending on what they read before it and even what they had for breakfast. It's often you'll see a story in their pages that doesn't seem to fit what they usually publish anyway.

Besides, writers are notoriously bad at judging their own work. That's why editors and agents and critique groups exist in the first place.

The only way to know for sure if an editor at any particular publication is going to accept or reject your work is to submit it. Stop trying to do their jobs for them. Do your job instead: write and submit.

That being said, this book is meant to curb the fear of rejection all writers face. So if saturating yourself in a particular publication boosts your confidence enough to submit your work to them, that's okay too. To help keep your budget under control in this process, check your local library for back issues, borrow copies from friends, or read their sample issues and stories online if the publication shares them.

PAY-TO-SUBMIT MODEL

Once upon a time, readers paid a lot of money for magazines that published fiction. Agents found up-and-coming writers this way. And magazines had plenty of cash to pay submissions editors to read through the slush pile with an eye for the next F. Scott Fitzgerald. This was how writers like Robert Heinlein got their start and paid their rent.

But technology has changed the way we consume content. Readers don't buy print magazines like they used to. That means publications don't have the funds to pay slush pile readers like they once could.

Enter the pay-to-submit model. (Cue the angry outcry.) Writers don't love paying submissions fees. But many publications wouldn't be around for you to publish in if they didn't ask for one.

The reality is, everyone wants to be published in these magazines but not enough writers read them. That's too bad because those who do read them have a better sense of the industry.

Ultimately, you'll have to decide whether or not to submit to these magazines. Check reviews and do your research to avoid scams. But I hope you'll choose to submit to the legitimate ones when it works for you. Why?

- It's a small investment compared to the internships you might do to break into any career.

- The submissions fee often comes with a subscription to the magazine. There's no better way to understand what each magazine likes to publish than to read it.

- Publication in one of these quality magazines can easily launch your writing career.

My suggestion? Accept the shock, lament the state of the industry for a minute or two, rail against the injustice (quietly and inside your own head), adjust to the reality, and submit your story.

REJECTED STORIES

Waaaaait a dang minute! (record scratch) What if every publication I submit to rejects my story?

It's probably going to happen, even if you've published before. So take a deep breath and then...

The beauty of this system is that there's no reason to worry about rejection anymore, because there's always a new publication to send your story to. And there's always a new story to send to the previous publication.

With this strategy, it's only a matter of time before something hits and you're a published author.

What happens if the entire list of publications you submitted your story to sends you a rejection letter? Hey, they can't all be winners, which is why this strategy is so great. We don't leave our writing dreams in the hands of any one story or any one publication.

So retire that little rejection-magnet for six months. By then you'll ideally have twenty-four more stories under your belt. And you'll be that much more skilled at recognizing what maybe didn't work in this one.

That's when you can decide if there's something the story needs to make it irresistible to editors. You'll also know better by then if you want to bother to rework the story or write it off as a skills-building exercise. Because, hey, it's just one story of twenty-five, right? And you might be published by then anyway.

The more you submit, the more chances you'll get published. You've got nothing to lose.

SUBMISSIONS TOOLS

COVER LETTER WORKSHEET

1 THE PUBLICATION'S EDITOR

2 STORY TITLE + WORD COUNT

3 WHAT YOU LOVE ABOUT THE PUBLICATION

4 YOUR PREVIOUS PUBLICATIONS (IF ANY)

5 YOUR WRITING AWARDS + ACCOMPLISHMENTS

6 THE PUBLICATION'S SUBMISSION REQUIREMENTS

7 ABOUT YOU

SIMPLE COVER LETTERS WORK BEST

Here's how to use the worksheet to write yours:

1. Check the publication's website for the editor's name. Avoid using gendered titles like Mr., Mrs., and Miss. It's too easy to mistakenly choose the wrong one and offend the editor. To be safe, use the editor's first and last name instead, without a title. "Dear Editor" or even "Dear fiction readers of [Magazine Title]" can work well as a last resort if you genuinely can't track down the editor's name.

2. Round the word count to the nearest hundred words.

3. Why did you submit your story to this particular publication? Did you connect with a story they recently published? Sometimes it helps to share info like this, so they know you read their publication. This also helps to humanize you.

4. If you haven't published yet, don't let it deter you. Many magazines love discovering new talent. If you have published, list just your top few publications.

5. List only writing-related accomplishments here.

6. Use this as a checklist to ensure your submission complies with the publication's guidelines. For example, are there any special instructions for simultaneous submissions?

7. Is there anything about you, your experiences, or your work that directly relates to the story? For example, are you a rocket scientist submitting a story about space travel?

COVER LETTER TEMPLATE

[Editor's Name]
[Editor's Title]
[Publication Title]
[Publication Address]

Dear [Entry #1 from worksheet],

Please consider my story, "[story title from worksheet entry #2]" ([word count from worksheet entry #2]) for publication in [Publication Title].

[Here's a good place to mention what you love about their publication, if you choose.]

My previous publications include [your publications list from worksheet entry #4]. And [your list of writing accomplishments from worksheet entry #5].

[Here's a good place to mention any special qualifications you have that directly relate to your story from worksheet entry #7].

Sincerely,

[Your Name]
[Your URL if you have one]

SAMPLE COVER LETTER

Jane Smith
Editor
Best Literary Magazine
123 A Street
University Town, State, Zip

Dear Jane Smith,

Please consider my story, "My Best Short Story" (2000 words) for publication in *Best Literary Magazine*.

My previous publications include short stories in *The Sweeping Review* and *McSalty's*. And my story, "The Last Best Story" won first place in AmeriCon's Best Short Contest.

Thank you in advance for reading.

Sincerely,

John Jones
johnjones.com

SUBMISSIONS TRACKER

TITLE OF WORK	PUBLICATION/ MARKET	SIM SUBS OKAY?	DATE SENT	EXPECT REPLY BY	FOLLOWED UP ON	OUTCOME	DATE OF REPLY	NOTES

HOW TO USE YOUR SUBMISSIONS TRACKER

▼

1. Title of Work: Your story's title.

2. Publication/Market: The publication you submitted to.

3. Sim Subs Okay?: Some publications accept simultaneous submissions if you alert them when your submission is accepted elsewhere. Your submissions tracker will tell you which publications to contact when that happens.

4. Date Sent: The date you submitted your story.

5. Expect Reply By: The publication's website or submission guidelines often state how long it takes them to reply to a submission. Record the date here, so you know when to follow up.

6. Followed Up On: Keep track of the dates you checked in with the publication about your story. Make sure you wait until after the "expect reply by" date before your first follow-up.

7. Outcome: Was your story accepted? Rejected? Did they offer feedback?

8. Date of Reply: The date the publication accepted/rejected the story.

9. Notes: Anything of note about the process or publication.

AFTERWORD

▼

That's it! Everything you need to land your first (or next) publication.

So write a short story. Submit a short story. Repeat. Because there are only so many times you're going to hear "no" in a row. Simple in theory, as long as you do the work.

GRATITUDE

▼

Thank you to my team of beta readers—Annis Cassells, Kirsten Oliphant, Terry Redman, Andrew Martin, and Kevin Chidgey—who made this book better and more helpful with their invaluable feedback.

Thank you to my son and husband for their patience while I worked on this passion project. And to my husband again for his edits and feedback.

Thank you to Yi Shun Lai for her expert insights on cover letter best practices.

And thank you to Joan Raymond, who always finds the errors and typos my eye slides right over (and thus helps me hide my tells).

ABOUT THE AUTHOR

▼

Mandy Wallace is a freelance writer, blogger, and mentor to new writers. Her mentorship program, Blog Your Way to a Writing Career, takes new writers from unknown to published. Through Blog Your Way to a Writing Career, Mandy teaches her students how to write for an online audience and how to use simple marketing techniques to build a readership for themselves online. (One of her students just landed a seven-figure book and movie deal.)

Her writing community at mandywallace.com has been featured as one of The Write Life's 100 Best Websites for Writers three years running. It's where she shares writing tips, resources, product reviews, and industry interviews for 20k+ monthly readers.

Occasionally, she'll dust off her honors BA in English Lit for bios like this one.

She says writing success is about skills more than talent, tenacity more than luck, and habit more than willpower.

It's this simple but powerful outlook that encourages the new writers in her classes and online community to keep writing and keep getting published.

63601911R00144

Made in the USA
Middletown, DE
27 August 2019